*Endorsements*

From the first time I met Apostle Harvey, I knew she was going to be a world changer. She has a heart for people that is rarely seen in this society. She never let her pain from the past hinder the plan, the path the Father placed her on. What the enemy thought would stop her just launched her into a growing ministry. She watched Father God turn it around for good. She embodies the image of the Father's unconditional love. She is an example of triumph over the situations life throws at us. This book will help women from all walks of life find hope and attain a successful, beautiful life in Christ.

*Pastor Shari Gray*
Passion Ecclesia Church
China Grove, North Carolina

As a survivor of life's trials and tribulations, I believe *Heeled: Walking From Pain to Purpose* will certainly heal the lives of many who have suffered and are suffering. For the many that suffer in silence, this book will bring confirmation that there is hope beyond the hurt. This book is a reminder that despite our suffering, we are always on God's mind.

*Pastor Annette L. Fallin*
Fragrance of Faith Ministry, Inc.
Baltimore, Maryland

# *Heeled*

## WALKING FROM PAIN TO PURPOSE

### DR. LINDA HARVEY

EDITED BY
## NICOLE QUEEN

VISION PUBLISHING
HOUSE

ISBN: 978-1-955297-44-8 ( Paperback)

LCCN: 2023910005

Vision Publishing House
9103 Woodmore Centre #334
Lanham, MD 20706

www.vision-publishinghouse.com

*This book is a tapestry of creative expressions from women who paused to reflect, reveal, and rejoice! It is dedicated to every woman whose heels carried her through the most painful experiences to paths of purpose, victory, and fulfillment. The trauma of our past cannot dictate the glory of our future!*

*The beauty of a swan is not the splendor of her feathers,*
*but the strength of the song she sings.*

— DR. LINDA HARVEY

# Contents

# Foreword

Thirty years ago, I attended one of my church's outdoor services. The atmosphere was filled with high worship and the presence of the Lord manifested on the streets of Baltimore, MD. The music, the praise and worship, the clapping of hands, and the songs of praise drew attention from all directions, capturing the surrounding area. Both pedestrians and drivers stopped to enjoy the resounding sound of praise in the airwaves.

Amidst this incredible scene, my attention was captivated by a woman like no other. She and her husband had pulled over, and our eyes met. Little did I know that this encounter marked the beginning of a divinely ordained connection. Linda Harvey, a minister of the gospel, caught my gaze with her well-put-together appearance and a smile that drew me in. Without uttering a word, her presence spoke volumes. From that day forward, we became friends, confidants, sisters, and co-laborers in the ministry. As time went on, we discovered that we shared more in common than we initially realized.

Here we were, two remarkable women who embodied grace, elegance, and a deep love for the Lord. Both of us were attractive, educated, married, and blessed with daughters. Our devotion to God was unwavering, and we wholeheartedly served Him. Along our journey, we embraced our calling as pastors, ministering in a field that resonated with our own experiences. We fearlessly shared our stories of abuse, shame, pain, and depression, finding solace and strength in each other's company. Through tears and laughter, we uplifted and inspired one another. There were dark moments when neither of us wanted to continue, but God's intervention was undeniable. His divine hand had been upon our lives even before we were conceived.

Today, when you look at my beloved sister and friend, you cannot fathom the trials she has triumphed over. She is a conqueror and an overcomer. Apostle Harvey is not only highly educated but also an esteemed educator. Her words carry immense authority, reflecting her no-nonsense approach. Despite her firmness, she remains one of the most loyal, faithful, and loving women of God. Her unwavering integrity is beyond reproach.

Apostle Harvey's heart is drawn to the downtrodden— those who may be considered unlovable, even in their own eyes. She possesses a profound understanding of the various forms of abuse: sexual, mental, emotional, physical, and spiritual.

In her journey, she reached a point where she firmly believed that "greater is He that is in her than he that is in this world." This realization transformed her into a spiritual warrior, advocating for those who could not advocate for themselves. She refused to let her own pain and suffering be in vain, recognizing that "all things would work together for her good," as it brought glory to her Heavenly Father.

As Apostle Harvey walks in her own healing and deliverance, she continues to extend a helping hand to the hungry, provide clothing to the naked, and offer shelter to the homeless. She is aware of her divine calling and the anointing upon her life, walking out the principles outlined in Isaiah 61:1.

> *The Spirit of the Sovereign Lord is on me, because*
> *the Lord has anointed me to proclaim good news to*
> *the poor. He has sent me to bind up the brokenhearted,*
> *to proclaim freedom for the captives, and release from*
> *darkness for the prisoners...*
>
> — ISAIAH 61:1 KJV

In her determination to fulfill the assignment before her and bring this project to completion, Apostle Harvey made the decision not only to share her own testimony but also to enlist the testimonies of others who have triumphed over immense trauma and despair. What makes their stories truly beautiful is that they now walk in victory. Each contributor, like many of us, spent years dressing up, applying makeup, slipping into painful high heels, and wearing a mask throughout the day. However, in this book titled "Heeled: Walking From Pain to Purpose," they courageously peel back the layers of despair and pain. They unmask themselves and guide us through the valley, revealing the true essence of hope and restoration.

Apostle Harvey invites you to kick off your "heels" and let the healing process to begin. GOD has a plan for your life as well. She challenges you to be what GOD has called you to be. Apostle Linda has advised me, educated me, cried with me, encouraged me and challenged me to do the same. Woman of GOD, I love you and thank GOD for you daily.

Apostle Harvey invites you to kick off your "heels" and embrace the beginning of your healing journey. God has a divine plan for your life, too. She challenges you to step into the fullness of what God has called you to be. Personally, Apostle Harvey has provided me with guidance, education, shared tears, words of encouragement, and inspiring challenges. This book is an extension of her compassion towards you. Receive it willingly and be all that God has called you to be.

*Apostle Etta Banks*, Pastor
New Vision For Life Church
Baltimore, MD

Her life a painful stroll
Maybelline tears— a constant flow
Heart pierced, crushed, and slowly dimmed
She masked the pain felt deep within
Every step— a strain to maintain

*Like walking in stilettos...*

— Dr. Linda Harvey

Fooled you in my heels
Thought my life was all together
As I sipped in my satin slip
Fake smiles in stormy weather

Fooled you in my stilts
Sweetly camouflaged in guilt
Measured by my soulful swag
You missed the purse with the crying rags

Fooled you in my spikes
Taunted by my fear at night
Hidden treasure, yet concealed
Masked beauty to reveal

Fooled you in my tips
Gilded smile with painted lips
The opinions of others never matter
It's a healed heart that I'm after

— Dr. Linda Harvey

# The Pruning Years

## by Cheryl Sketers

I just left the contractor's office after signing the contract for my new home. For three years, I have been trying to decide where to live and what to do. Now suddenly, I know.

One day on Google, while looking for something other than homes for a change, an advertisement popped up: "New homes on the way!" I glanced over and thought nothing of it. Later that night, the ad came to my mind over and over. The next day, I said, "Okay, I will read over the ad seriously this time."

The next thing I knew, I was driving to the construction site and had a conversation with the sales manager. It was a polite conversation; I was shown good virtual pictures of the future community. All looked inviting. However, I still needed more time to think it over. After a few days, that same nagging started again. I cannot explain it. I thought I really heard something saying, "Go." I said aloud, "Okay."

I went to tour the model. Just like that, I got up, took a break from work, and drove to the model. As I walked in, I was greeted and provided with a detailed tour of the home. I was very pleasantly surprised. Just one thing: it was not exactly what I wanted, but it was far more than I expected. Now what? I do not know.

Let me get back to work.

For the next two days, the nagging started again, and I ignored it. I had other things to think about that took priority, or so I thought. The phone suddenly rang. I did not recognize the number, but for some reason, I answered. It was the sales office.

"Hi, just checking back! We only have two left, and I do not want you to miss out." All of a sudden, I felt different. I thought, *God, is this You?* I said, "Okay, but I am still deciding and have yet to talk with a loan officer." She said, "No worries. I can connect you with our loan officer."

Next thing you know, I was connected. I gave the mandatory information for qualification, and within no time, the loan officer said, "Okay, what do you want to do next? We are here for you."

After I hung up the phone, I sat back and sat still. I thought, *God, is this You? This is surreal.* I started reflecting over the past decades. I never realized the many life challenges I endured. I never had a chance to, really— until now. I can still remember being told, "If you walk out of your marriage home, you will never get another." They did not care that it would be unhealthy if I stayed. They did not care that I had no choice but to leave.

When God blessed me with my beautiful child, the woman I thought I was vanished. A whole new warrior arose. Man, I was something else. *Superwoman!* I smile just thinking about it. I was ready for it all. I had zero tolerance for foolishness. I was all business, and truly not the one to play with. I laugh now, but certainly not then— *certainly* not then. Let me stop for a second here, as I need a moment to reflect.

*Goodbye, marriage.*
*Goodbye, beautiful home.*

I went from wife to mom— *single* mom— a title I never thought I would have. It went from mortgage to rent, just like that. All I worked hard for was gone. I repeated the family taboo. The only difference was that Mom taught me what took decades for her to learn. "Get out and leave early. Do not stay like I did," she used to say. She showed me what she thought she did not have. *Strength!* She is still the strongest woman I know. In some way, the new life was working. I was starting to see the light again. I was starting to smile again. No more chaos! I have hope! I pushed forward, trusting that God would help me.

Pending my divorce, I was told, "You will not qualify for a home. You now have a bankruptcy, and your situation is not settled." Although that was amazing, none of that mattered. I was approved and moving forward, against all odds. I was a homeowner, against all odds. How? They said it would never happen. I survived the divorce, but it cost me something, and I am not talking about money. God replaced my home with a new home. My new challenge was making peace with the ending, and now figuring out how to co-parent, regardless of the challenges. I was living for someone other than me now.

I learned so much from that experience. No, it certainly was not what I hoped for, but it was more than I expected in many other ways— negative and positive. Perhaps it was the test of many more, or was God forcing me to grow up? I pushed forward. It was tough, but I had to do it. I survived. We survived.

When you think you have survived one situation, oftentimes you do not realize it was to prepare you for the next journey. Becoming a delicate part of your parents' life when they can no longer make decisions or care for themselves is an honor, yet hurts more than words can say. You see, the person who used to be a pillar of strength is now weak and dependent. The provider who never wanted to feel weak is weak and mad about it. While they try to accept their new truth, I look on and wonder... *is this payback?*

You try to forget what you saw growing up, as you stare down at the hospital bed. Regardless of the ugliness of the past, I did everything with honor. I received the utmost support from my parents. It is amazing. How did they do it? I was always supported. The love I felt from my parents molded me significantly. I thank God for my parents. I am grateful for the life lessons learned. I never realized how those lessons would help me later, and how their hardships made me stronger, while preparing me for my future.

Everything was changing. My world was now deprived of four members of my immediate family. My brother— I still can't. Grief has become a permanent challenge now.

These days of reminiscing are a necessity. *I miss you, Mom. You're still the strongest woman I know.*

Well... enough reflections.

What a day. I'm a homeowner! Good morning! Happy Saturday! I start each day by reading my daily Scripture verse. I routinely get my two glasses of water in first, then my coffee. My daily goal is sixty-four ounces of water. As I start my day, I can't help but think about how yesterday flowed. I think about the events of the day and all of the future steps of becoming a homeowner, once again.

Never say what you can't do because life has a way of showing you, otherwise. You start off looking at others' lives, saying how, and the next thing you know, you are asking yourself the same question.

I call the past four years of my life the pruning years. Why? It really feels like I have been purposely isolated. No, not COVID-19 isolated, not remote work isolated, but God isolated.

A few years back, I moved to a new state because of my career. I was away from all I knew. My options were really none: severance or move? So, I guess I'm moving. I sold my home.

I started all over again.

Who would have thought? Each day, I said, "Okay, Lord. I love you. I trust you. But why? What do you want from me?" I feel like I have the weight of the world on my shoulders. It's heavy. How can I ever retire, starting over yet again?"

I continued to push forward and move ahead. Excitement set in. My child was now a college graduate. The move... the sacrifice... I would do it again. I am so proud! Thank you, Lord! Being a mother is more than I can ever say. I am grateful. I made sacrifices repeatedly to see this day. I have a different mindset now.

Each challenge has taken something from me, but has also given me something in return. I could be bitter, but for some reason, I am not. It's so strange because I used to be. I cannot recall the day it did not matter anymore. I am not where I thought I would be. Every now and then, I get agitated, but I shake it off. I have more peace now than ever before. Is that strange?

Quiet time is my best time now. I feel like I'm a seed slowly growing into a person I am unaware of. The past is slowly taking its rightful place. I don't hang on to it like I used to. More importantly, I don't want to. I am letting go of people who don't fit, as well. Conversations are not the same anymore, and I feel good being alone. I prefer being alone. I now understand the difference between being alone and lonely. I'm not lonely. I feel like a warrior is growing inside of me, again. How is this? Am I blossoming? When you endure challenges in life, you get to a point where your peace is so precious.

During the pruning years, God helped me work on my anger and bitterness; He went straight to my roots of darkness. It took years because the roots were deeply embedded, but it was my safe place. It was my place of solitude for a while. I was ready for a change, but I decided to make the decision this time. Was it vain to think it was just me? I didn't know anymore. I didn't even care because I knew God was guiding me. I knew God loved me.

I smiled to myself and said, "You're okay." You are a: survivor, daughter, sister, ex-wife, mother, provider, power of attorney, caregiver, regional manager, sister-in-Christ, domestic violence volunteer, and now a leader in church serving on the domestic violence ministry— but more importantly, a woman growing in God."

Was it because I listened and made decisions I was afraid of, but made anyway? Challenges taught me to stay focused and move, while being afraid. What does fear get anyone? It does not mean I was not shaken, it just meant that I had to keep moving, though I felt afraid and uncertain.

Today, I am in awe of God's favor. He not only blessed me with a beautiful, new smart home, but He also blessed me with love. I have a Man of God who adores me for me! Won't He do it!

# *About the Author*

Cheryl Sketers pursued her higher education at Virginia State University. She is a regional manager with an over 34 years of experience, works alongside the executive team of a Fortune 500 company. Cheryl is responsible for managing and building superior customer service. Cheryl is a powerful force in the workplace and uses her positive attitude and strong work ethic to encourage others to work hard and succeed. She has been promoted several times and has received numerous awards for team performance, high metrics, overall performance, and execution.

Cheryl is a faith-driven woman dependent on God's guidance. She taught Sunday school for children aged 10 and under and served as a member of the Church Finance team.

Cheryl is a trained Domestic Violence volunteer that builds tools for women and girls in need. In October 2022, her Domestic Violence submission was approved by her pastor, who publicly announced to the church congregation that she would be leading the newly established Domestic Violence Ministry. Her first Domestic Violence event took place on April 16, 2023, featuring a guest speaker from Safe Harbor. Cheryl is dedicated to helping women by offering the necessary resources and education. In the near future, she aims to collaborate with the Missions Ministry to provide care kits for women who are forced to leave their homes with nothing. She is in the process of preparing for her second event that's scheduled for October 2023.

Cheryl is deeply grateful for all the recognition and accolades she has received, but she wants to be known for something beyond those accomplishments. Her greatest achievement, one that cannot be measured by awards, is being a mother. It is a role she cherishes with the utmost honor and pride. Raising a well-rounded and educated Black young man brings her immense joy and fulfillment. It is a beautiful journey that she embraces wholeheartedly.

The blessing of having key sources of strength is the backbone to Cheryl's determination to succeed. Her personal motto is: *Never give up! God has His arms wrapped around you. Just accept His love!*

# Hope Beyond the Hurt

## by Latasha Hutt

As I look back over the last twenty years of my life, I can truly say that I have encountered many challenges that have changed the course of my journey— some by chance and some by choice. I know everything happens for a reason, and God will indeed make way for me to be victorious through my trials.

One of my favorite songs to listen to when I cannot seem to understand life's struggles is "You Made a Way" by Tasha Cobbs-Leonard. That song ministers to the very core of my heart and uplifts me every time I hear it. Whatever situations I encounter, I know if I truly hand it over to God and believe in Him, He will make a way.

Like many others, pain has made its mark on my life— painful experiences that have involved family, friends, personal relationships, motherhood, and even my career. Each circumstance has taught me ways to navigate through my pain. I have pushed through many hurtful experiences on my own, not because I had to or was forced to, but because I didn't want to feel like a burden to others. I am a very private person, so most of my pain became secrets that I would rather not address with anyone but God. I tucked them down on the inside, thinking that it was the best place to keep them.

I now know that "going at it alone" is not always the best answer.

However, I can say that going through some situations alone has taught me not to trust man, but God. Those private and secret moments allowed me to rely on the one who could truly help me mend my hurt. As I pushed through my struggles, each experience taught me how to self-heal while becoming closer to God.

## HURT BY CHANCE

Anything that happens by chance is something that happens without a plan or intent. It is something that you are not quite prepared for or expecting. Many things can happen by chance, but I always thought of those things as good things, like winning a car or a free trip. But the by-chance event that happened in my life brought tears of uncertainty. Learning of my daughter's disability was a big turning point for me as a parent.

My daughter was diagnosed with autism when she was a toddler. Of course, like most, I knew other parents that had children with autism, but now it was me. I never really took the time to consider what I would do if put in that position, but now, here I was facing it. This was my first encounter with fully trusting God. I have always loved God and had faith in Him, but this time, my trust in Him was deeper than I had ever experienced. I knew that I had to turn to Him because He was the only one that could help me through how I was feeling. I was heartbroken and blamed myself for my daughter's diagnosis. It seemed like everything happened so fast. One day she was perfect in every way; the next, she lost everything she once knew. I couldn't understand why she began to change right before my eyes. I went through so many emotions watching my daughter cognitively decline. All I could do was pray and ask God to guide me. This changed the course of my journey and helped push me to my purpose in God. I had to trust that God had my back.

We all know the scripture, "The LORD is close to the brokenhearted and saves those who are crushed in spirit" (Psalm 34:18, NIV). God knows I was crushed and broken. Even today, I keep that scripture near my heart because God never left me. Through all the self-blame, frustration, confusion, and disappointments, He stayed with me. Instead of becoming angry with the world, I turned to God and gave

Him all my tears and prayer requests. He never went back on His Word; He was and has been with me every step of the way.

To give you a little background, my daughter was a "normal" child, full of love and laughter. I still remember her standing in front of the television, singing her favorite songs and dancing along to them. Her favorite song was "I'm Not Perfect" by Laurie Berkner. She would sing that song for hours at a time. One day, I noticed she wasn't singing like she used to. She began to make many noises instead of singing and talking. After several doctor visits, she was diagnosed with Autism at the age of two and a half. Over the next few years, I witnessed a consistent decline. She turned mostly nonverbal, only saying one- or two-word sentences. I remember so many nights I cried to myself because I felt like I had failed her. I didn't want to tell anyone how I felt because I didn't want to share how disappointed I was in myself. I just kept asking, "How could this healthy child lose all verbal communication?" My heart was crushed. As a parent, you want to save your children from all harm, but I could only sit back and watch it all play out. I wanted my daughter back— the one who knew all the words to her favorite songs, smiled, called my name, and danced around with pure joy. It was definitely many emotions to take in at one time.

I constantly prayed and asked God to provide me with the answers. I remember asking Him, "How can I care for this child? What am I supposed to do to help her?" I was not equipped to understand her needs. As I prayed and prayed, God spoke to me and told me that He qualified the chosen. At that moment, I didn't understand what He meant by that, but I trusted Him enough to accept His answer. Although I had doubts about my parenting, I took it one day at a time because I knew what God had said. I knew He would give me what I needed to care for her.

Fast-forward to today, my daughter has graduated High School! To God be the glory! There are still so many hurdles that we will have to face, and that's okay. The important thing I have learned throughout the years is that *everything* happens for a reason. Jeremiah 29:11 (NIV) says, "For I know the plans I have for you,' declares the LORD, 'plans to prosper you and not to harm you, plans to give you hope and a future."

The truth is, God had my life story all planned out. Now, I understand that this did not just happen. God chose me for this assignment. Even though I was brokenhearted and crushed spiritually when I first learned of my daughter's disability, I continued to seek God and never forgot His promise to me that He would qualify me. He has done just that over the years. I am truly thankful that He has equipped me to care for such a beautiful child. We have had some challenging days, which is expected, but I have truly enjoyed the journey that we have been on. She has taught me what unconditional love looks like without saying a word. The connection I have with her is nothing short of a miracle.

This journey has given me a greater appreciation for people and God. I became closer to God because motherhood allowed me to rely solely on Him for guidance, strength, and confirmation. He blessed me with a second daughter shortly after my first. She has grown up to be my backbone and support. She cares for her older sister with grace— no judgment, no questions— just love. She is an additional gift from God to her sister and me— my ram in the bush. Man, oh man, has God equipped me!

## HURT BY CHOICE

Have you ever heard of the sayings: *'Life is what you make it'* and *'Every choice is your own?'* I really didn't pay attention to those sayings too much growing up, but I have to say that they are really true; every choice you make in life is truly your own. Personally, I always made the choice to make others happy. Most of the time, I would put others' happiness in front of my own. I never complained about it because I felt that I was doing the right thing. But through life's experiences, I have learned that I need to make choices that also benefit me. Many choices I made helped others but were not the best for me.

My choices have caused me disappointment, frustration, and hurt. As I mentioned, throughout my teenage years, I always tried to be the perfect friend. That same energy followed me into adulthood. I constantly wanted to make others happy and work hard to earn their loyalty and friendship. So, I worked overtime to be what I thought the people around me wanted and needed.

Philippians 2:3 (NIV) says, "Do nothing out of selfish ambition or vain conceit. Rather, in humility, value others above yourselves." I live by this scripture. I put others before myself because I want to see them do well and show them that I have an unwavering love for them. I always thought having such a giving spirit was a blessing and a curse. I often asked God, *Why am I so softhearted, forgiving, and caring toward others?* God quickly showed me that He loved that very part of me. No matter what, He did not want me to change myself. So now, I tell people this is who I am, and God prefers me this way.

As I experienced hurt through different relationships, I would often blame myself for anything that went wrong. I would cry and get upset. As I mentioned in my first experience, I had the same defense, although this was a different kind of hurt. I shut down and kept it all inside. I did my best to self-heal and believe solely in God for peace of mind and a mended heart. It felt better to shut it all away. Deep down inside, I knew that I could only control myself and no one else. I asked God to give me the strength to cope with the feelings of hurt and move forward. I became closer to God as I healed through silence. I offered Him my broken pieces, and He offered me His hand to hold as He molded and reconstructed me. I truly thank God for each part of my reconstruction.

I can recall one encounter with a friend that left me broken. I didn't understand what I had done wrong. In my mind, I had done everything right. I did everything I could to make them happy. But to be truthful, I never felt like I could measure up to what this person wanted or needed, so doing everything right was a far cry. I lost myself trying to serve them. I felt like I was in control of the situation and knew what I was doing. I thought I was being a true friend, but the real truth was that the whole situation had control of me. I was no longer serving God the way I should have been, but rather serving man, trying to make sure I did everything right for them— not God, not me, but them. In the end, none of my hard work or loyalty mattered. I was left broken and disappointed. All of those feelings came from the choices that I made.

Looking back, I now see that I was showing up as a lesser version of what God called me to be. I was showing up based on man-made assumptions and expectations, not really being true to myself. God never designed me to operate that way. My choices were not right, and I was hurting because of it. Changing the past is impossible, so I moved forward, acknowledging the mistakes that I had made. As the famous Tony Robbins once said, "Change only happens when the pain of staying the same is greater than the pain of change." I knew I could only do better by not making the same mistakes again, so change had to happen.

Even though I knew I wanted to move on from my bad choices, I still felt overwhelmed by all the changes I needed to make. I was ashamed to even pray to God about my situation because I knew I had put myself there. After months of crying secretly, I finally cried out to God and asked Him to teach me how to become unchained from my place of vulnerability. God began to show me my weaknesses, and I started to listen to Him. I knew I had to listen to get out of the slump that I was in. As I opened myself completely to God, He started transforming my hurt into healing.

My first step was finding myself worthy of whom God said I was. The experiences made me think that I wasn't a good or loyal enough friend and didn't deserve love and respect. But the devil is a liar. God had to pick me up from my mess to show me that I am wonderfully and fearfully made. And anyone who deserves to be in my life should be able to respect and honor my presence in their lives the right way.

Secondly, I had to learn to forgive the ones who hurt me. I wanted people to hurt the way they hurt me. At the time, in my mind, I didn't feel that people should do things to others and get away with it. But God says, "I see it all, and vengeance is mine." I had to learn to leave everything in God's hands. Instead of asking God to give them what I thought they deserved, I asked God to heal the people who hurt me so they could be transformed and never hurt again.

As I move forward, I know that I cannot change people. The day I started praying for healing for myself and those who hurt me, God started to heal me and set me free. Let's be clear, the only way you can get this type of peace and deliverance is through growing an unshakeable relationship with God. It took months of prayer for me to be able to say, "God, I wish them a very prosperous life," and actually mean it. But I reached that point when I humbled myself, listened to God, read the Word, and examined myself. Only then did I truly get the full release of God's glory upon my life.

## UNDERSTANDING THROUGH EXPERIENCES

Yes, I have experienced hurt by chance and choice. My daughter's diagnosis happened by chance; it was not planned or expected. The personal relationships I engaged in were by choice, and every decision I made, I had to live with. In both situations, I encountered hurt and disappointment. Through understanding the process of life, I learned that we, as human beings, might not have control over some things we go through, while in other situations, we do. Regardless of the circumstance, God is still God and will be right by our sides. Experiences like these have helped me become closer to God. I now understand that He is my source of refuge in my storms.

So, if I had to answer the question, '*How did these situations change me?*' I would say, '*Tremendously!*' I have the utmost respect and empathy for parents raising children with exceptionalities. It takes a great deal of patience and love. I also have a better understanding of people who hurt others. They, too, are loving people who only need God to put them back on the right path. There was a purpose in all of the experiences I went through. God allowed these experiences in my life to help me grow personally and spiritually. I have accepted God as my provider, healer, comforter, and friend. I found myself because God gave me His grace and mercy every day. I don't know where I would be if it were not for Him.

These experiences are my own, but I know many people have stories that align with mine. If you allow me to leave you with a thought, it would be this: Embrace your life experiences— the good, the bad, and the ugly! Always remember that God has written your story. He knows the beginning and the end. He has graciously allowed us to live this life, to go through each chapter, and enjoy all He has for us. Always remember that He is with you. He will never leave you nor forsake you! Let God hold your hand through the challenges of life. Sometimes you don't need to be rescued from the challenges. You need Him to walk alongside you to guide you. I promise that at the end of the storm, you can look back and find self-growth or a learned lesson. And always, always remember that there is hope beyond your hurt. God bless you on your personal journey from pain to purpose!

# *About the Author*

Latasha, born Latasha Marie Hutt, was raised on the Eastern Shore of Virginia in Accomack County. She received her education through the Accomack County Public School system and graduated from Chincoteague High School in 2003. In 2015, she earned a Bachelor's Degree in Education from Ashford University, and in 2018, she obtained a Master's Degree in Special Education from Grand Canyon University. Currently, Latasha is pursuing a Master's Degree in School Counseling from Liberty University. She is a mother, Licensed Education Professional, and a mentor and advocate for youth. But most importantly, she is a child of God dedicated to helping young women and families throughout her community.

Having faced her own personal challenges, Latasha is now driven by a passion to provide counseling and support to young women who have experienced low self-esteem, stress, and emotional struggles. She desires to work closely with other women of God to positively impact the community and help bring resources to women in need of support. Using her educational background, personal experiences, and sharing God's word, her goal is to empower other women to move forward in their personal and spiritual lives.

Latasha found her way back to Christ at Restoration Outreach Healing Ministry in Onancock, Virginia, where she is currently a member. She has partnered with other women in the ministry to create an outreach program. Latasha firmly believes that all women, regardless of their background history, can lead a healthy life physically, mentally, and spiritually. Her inspiration behind writing this chapter stems from her own experiences and the discovery of hope and purpose that unfolded throughout her personal journey.

# Breathe: Healing Through My Breakthrough

## by Letitia Council

O n the night of August 15, 2019, I was faced with a tragedy that I was forced to face. My oldest daughter was in a motor vehicle accident with life-threatening injuries. She sustained a hematoma to the front right side of her head, which caused traumatic brain injury. The tragedy caused me to be face-to-face with pain, hurt, and frustration.

As a mother, it was something on a level that I could never imagine. Pain from trauma will have you feeling like you will never see victory. It will have you questioning if you will ever allow God to help you heal. The truth is that you must be disciplined and go through the process of pain, hurt, and frustration.

I had to sit and listen to the doctor tell my husband and me that based on his experience and the severity of our daughter's injury, her quality of life would soon be endless. As parents, we don't ever think about preparing a homegoing service for our children. God heard our cries. But before He heard our cries, He already knew His plans for Ja'Nasia and how He was going to comfort me through my pain.

*"For I know the thoughts that I think toward you, saith the*

*Lord, thoughts of peace, and not of evil, to give you an expected end."*

— JEREMIAH 29:11 (KJV)

When we are going through challenges, we tend to mask our pain because we don't want sympathy. However, masking up doesn't help your pain.

The trauma processing settled just a little bit. I had to walk past Nasia's room to get to my room. I wasn't ready to walk past her room and peek in her room like I did every day. The first time I went back home after the accident, I went to shower. While in the shower, behind closed doors, I cried like a baby. Now, I had to be face-to-face with surviving the hurt and pain.

When I was faced with the tragedy, I couldn't understand for the life of me, *why* this had to happen to my family and me. I wasn't living the best godly life at the time of the accident. My daughter wasn't making the best decisions as a young adult, but I just couldn't believe we came face-to-face with a tragedy. Each day, while my daughter was in the hospital fighting for her life, we had to sit still and be patient. Every day and night, the reports from the doctors sounded like they were the same, but God was the narrator of the report. Day after day, I had to process the challenge. I remained strong for my family, but on the inside, I was torn to pieces. My husband could see in my eyes that what we were facing had shattered my heart, and there wasn't much he could do to repair the shattered pieces.

The hurt and pain I felt inside were masked up on the outside. I felt that if I remained strong and silenced the true hurt and pain on the inside, our daughter would feel that I was fighting right alongside her.

We all have heard the saying, "God allows things to happen in our lives for a reason." Truth be told, at that time, I didn't know whether to believe in that statement or not! Now that I have had two years to fully process what took place on the night of August 15, 2019, I believe that God allowed the accident to happen to not only give my daughter a second chance at life— although different from the one she lived prior to the accident— but to also save my life!

Now I know many won't understand this following statement, but truth be told, God saved a mother and daughter at the same time through one tragedy. God will do what He needs to do to get our attention. If you are a Believer, you would know that to be true.

When you have the weight of trauma on your shoulders and the everyday challenges of life, you somehow seem to push each day of weight under the rug, just to add more weight on top of what you already have. We don't like to face our pain. We mask the pain and walk around smiling, knowing we are hurting inside. Hurt people hurt people. So, every hour of the day that we mask up the pain, we aren't only hurting ourselves— we are also hurting those we love the most.

As I journeyed through the daily pain, especially as the caregiver to my daughter, I had to smile, cry in silence, scream in the other room, and find things to help ease the moment of the pain. I've never been the woman to share my painful days because I didn't want anyone to feel sorry for me. Not only was it pain from the tragedy that hurt, but it was also pain as a mother, knowing I couldn't do anything to help change the fight my daughter was in.

As a mother, we have always saved the day in our children's eyes, but this time, I had to do something differently. I had to increase my prayer life and allow God to lead the way and do what He does. Amid all the pain and hurt inside, you become a different person you don't even seem to recognize. You lose who you once were, feel hopeless, and may even feel alone (even though you are surrounded by the best support team ever). I still couldn't help but think how someone could do something like this and keep on going! I carried the pain of my husband and our children.

On September 12, 2019, my phone rang; it was the best news ever! I received the call that my daughter had been approved to be transported to rehab! It was exciting. We were finally on our way to Recovery Level 2!

Yet, the pain was still there. Nasia still couldn't talk, but she understood what I was saying to her, as I got her dressed and ready for the transport team to come. She was finally being discharged from the hospital.

Pain causes anxiety. Although I was excited that she was being discharged, I was worried about her being in the ambulance by herself, as it would be her first time being transported since being admitted. When Nasia arrived at rehab, which was a two-hour drive, we learned that her body had spiked a temperature! I had to take deep breaths because I was already nervous about her being transported. Then, finding out Nasia's status upon arrival had me heated. Again, this was another hurtful moment where I couldn't do anything but be patient, wait, and pray that nothing would cause a setback in Nasia's recovery.

Once the care team could get Nasia's body temperature back to normal, I was at ease. It was almost like the hurt and pain kept building up, and I kept hiding it! My culture taught me to be strong no matter what. Although it had already been almost a month post-tragedy, the hurt, pain, and frustration remained. The broken pieces of me always remained behind closed doors. It wasn't that I was ashamed to show my brokenness; it was because my daughter was in there fighting for her life that I felt the need to remain strong.

When we hide our brokenness due to survival mode, we don't get the chance to feel the hurt and pain. I was afraid of the true pain that came with the trauma we faced every day.

As each day went by, I continued to bury my pain. I didn't realize how much I was hurting myself. Once my daughter was discharged from the hospital and admitted to rehabilitation, it felt like the pain had eased up. When you're on the journey of brain recovery, you don't truly know which way the process will go, and if the survivor will recover.

Each day I prayed to God, asking Him to strengthen Nasia's vocal cords so we could hear her voice. When the day would end and night would fall, and still no voice, no movement *still*, I'd be hurt. However, I would still hide it with a smile because God had given our daughter a second chance when He could've called her home the night of the accident.

On September 23, 2019, when the rehabilitation doctor came into Nasia's room, he said, "Nasia will be discharged on October 3, 2019!" I said, "That is next week!"

I can't tell you how relieved I was! I dismissed the pain, hurt, and frustration of not knowing the prognosis due to the injury. My wound was still there and wasn't healed properly, but I didn't allow the hurt to consume me.

October 3, 2019 finally arrived! Oh, what a relief it was knowing Nasia would be coming home for the first time since she left on the night of August 15, 2019.

The whole process of nurturing Nasia back to health with the help of God was exciting! Yes, it was exciting, but I masked the pain at that time. I would cry at night because I was hurting. Now, the hurt was because I still hadn't heard my daughter's voice. She was back home readapting to her environment. Nasia didn't recognize she was home right away. It took her about a month to realize she was back home. Her brain injury affected her right frontal side. Being home became familiar to her because we would get her out of bed every day and wheel her to the front room.

Truth is, I masked my pain for two years. Masking my pain became easy, and identifying the hurt became silenced. I was in survival mode. Once God answered the question I asked Him in August 2019— *How can I help the youth?* — I began to recognize my purpose while being a caregiver, wife, and mother.

In January 2020, God gave me The Nasia Foundation. That was the answer to my question in August 2019. A month later, The Nasia Foundation was conceived. That's when it hit me— what my purpose truly was.

On April 27, 2020, *The Nasia Foundation* was birthed. Not knowing about running a nonprofit, I trusted God because I knew He would help me walk in my Godly purpose. And He did just that!

Walking from pain to purpose in God was a challenge. The challenge of returning to where the pain began and facing the daily assignments caused a lot of hurt, tears, and self-reflection. I knew it was necessary to bury the pain because God had something *greater* in store for me. God knew there was much pain hiding behind the mask. There was more than one mask I was wearing.

When unpacking the pain to walk in your godly purpose, the levels to unpacking your pain are necessary. To accept your purpose in God, you must unmask the levels of pain not only for yourself, but also for the ones God has called you to help.

I couldn't help but think about what if my daughter didn't have a brain injury; what would she be doing, or where would she be? Those were challenges that I had to face, knowing I would never get a chance to have those questions answered.

Just when I thought I could walk away from the pain, there were still unknown, hurtful answers. Nasia still couldn't speak verbally, so she couldn't answer any of my questions about that night. However, she was able to communicate non-verbally. Though I was grateful for her improvements since coming home to be in our care, I still had those questions. Unanswered questions are also hurtful.

There were many days after I said, "Yes, God, I will carry out my purpose that you have assigned to me," that I still carried the hurt and pain. When people would see me in person, speak with me over the phone, or even comment on the live videos that I would do on social media, they would often say, "You are so strong!" But what they didn't see were those moments when I would cry behind closed doors. I wouldn't allow anyone to see me in my brokenness because I didn't want sympathy. I wanted someone to understand how I was feeling on the inside.

In most cases, even my husband didn't see those broken moments behind closed doors. I would cry in my bathroom when no one was home, except Nasia and me. Those were the moments I would ask God why, yet He still chose me!

Although Nasia couldn't talk, I knew she could feel it when I hurt. Seeing her with a brain injury and not being able to live the life we thought she should be living still hurt. Caring for and loving Nasia didn't give me time to truly release my hurt and pain.

As I was getting over the pain, my life took an unexpected turn right after I said *yes* to God. On the morning of April 25, 2021, I completed Nasia's daily routine care and administered her medication. I was standing at her dresser with my back turned, and God showed me a vision of my husband and me standing by a casket. I immediately turned around, looked at Nasia, shook my head, and said, "No, not my baby! God is not about to call her home." So, I proceeded to do what I was doing, but the vision came again. I shook my head again and said *no*!

I walked over to Nasia, kissed her, and said, "Mommy is about to go get dressed for church." On that morning, I was supposed to be at church by 9:30 a.m. Before I left the house, I said, "Okay, Nasia, Mommy and your sister are about to go to church. Your dad and brother are here with you." She gave me a slight head nod. I said, "I'll see you when I get back home." The time was now 9:45 a.m.

When I arrived at church, it was a little after 10:00 a.m. I walked into the church to assist with my assignment for that Sunday. My phone rang, and my husband told me I needed to get back home. I asked him, "Why, what's wrong?" He said, "Babe, I just need you to get back home."

The night before (Saturday night), God had shown me, spoke to me, and told me that I would have a 911 call that next day (which was Sunday). God showed me that my cell phone would ring, and it would read *Husband*.

That's when my heart dropped, and I began to cry because I could no longer hold back my tears. I went to my apostle and informed him of the call. My cousin walked out of the church with me. I pulled myself together and drove myself and my youngest daughter back home. The entire drive home felt like I wasn't driving fast enough.

Once I arrived on my street, my heart dropped even more. I saw the fire truck and the ambulance. My dad and husband were standing outside, waiting for my arrival. Paramedics were in our home performing CPR on our daughter. When I walked in my house, tears were rolling, and the pain that I thought was at ease was at an all-time high again.

Our lives were altered, yet again. God called Ja'Nasia home to rest in His arms at the age of twenty. Nasia had gained her heavenly wings and her reward. Now that was pain and hurt on another level! Ja'Nasia was my firstborn. There I was, full of pain that only God could ease.

During the whole process of planning our daughter's homegoing service, I was trying to be strong, again. That pain hurt— I mean *hurt*! The hardest part about the homegoing service was closing the casket. The pain and hurt were unbearable. That's when I began to experience myself suffocating while trying to breathe.

After months of feeling like I was suffocating, God reminded me of His promise and purpose He entrusted me with. January 2022 came, and I felt empty. I've never felt like that before. We were in a new year, and I was without my daughter. I cried and talked to God numerous times. In February, I had my second breakdown, and that's when my mentor and spiritual midwife said to me just minutes apart, "Do you think it's time to seek counseling?" My response was *yes*!

The week before I began my counseling, God spoke to me and said, "Strength like no other reaches to me." God spoke that to me repeatedly. While He was speaking, He gave me the strength to break down Nasia's bed. Once I completed the breakdown of the bed, I heard God say, "Now, you can begin to heal!"

I began counseling two weeks later. That was a difficult decision, but I knew I needed to seek counseling to walk from pain into God's purpose *fully* this time. Walking from pain to purpose in God has allowed me to realize that masking up the pain can't go with me into my *now*, nor could I take the pain into my *new*.

After experiencing the pain and going through the process of trusting God and unpacking the pain, it hasn't changed my heart toward God negatively. However, it has increased my love deep down inside for God. I am beyond proud of myself for taking the necessary steps for my better well-being, so that I may serve those God has assigned to me and be able to move forward in my organization effectively without compromising God's purpose within me.

Don't let your pain cause you to abort your purpose because of your emotions and feelings of fear and rejection. You don't have the authority to dismiss the plan God predestined over your life before you were in your mother's womb. March forth— the world is waiting for *you*!

# About the Author

*Four-time #1 Amazon Bestselling Author, Inspirational Speaker,*
*Certified Life Coach, Certified Christian Mental Health Specialist, &*
*Non-Profit Founder*

Inspired by a genuine desire to help others, Letitia Council, Founder and President of The Nasia Foundation, is a woman on a mission. She serves as a Traumatic Brain Injury & Caregiver Advocate, passionately sharing her story and the reason behind her endeavors. Letitia uplifts women, empowering them to rise above the ashes of their trauma. Throughout her journey, she has been fortunate to contribute to various organizations that provide support to those in need. Letitia is not only a published author but has also been featured in four anthologies. Currently, she is part of two anthologies: *I am Tamar: Come out of Hiding* and *Heeled: Walking from Pain to Purpose.* She has an Associate of Occupational Science Degree in Medical Assisting from Tidewater Tech. She has also made appearances on notable platforms such as the Power and Grace Leaders Talk Show, BIG Mind Entertainment Real Notes Talk Show, Coast Live Show, and Voyage ATL Magazine. Letitia is the founder of Women on the Move Conference and Butterfly Moms Support Group. Additionally, she owns Letitia Council, LLC. Letitia is a loving, caring, and devoted wife, having celebrated 11 years of marriage with her incredibly supportive husband. As a mother of five children, Letitia cherishes the memory of their oldest daughter, Ja'Nasia Miller, a Traumatic Brain Injury Angel, who transitioned on April 25, 2021. Letitia now proudly identifies herself as a Butterfly Mom.

## Awards & Recognition 2023:
*Phenomenon Woman-My Sister Keeper 2023*
*Bully Magazine-Pain to Power Award August 2023*

## Nominations & Awards:
*Nonprofit Leader & Health Wellness- Sisters Leaders October 2022*
*Nonprofit of the Month- Turn Key November 2021*
*Nonprofit of the Year- Black Brand October 2021*
*Nonprofit Leader & Health Wellness-Sisters Leaders August 2021*

## ACHI Magazine Nominations 2022:
*Woman on the Rise*
*Woman of Influence*
*Nonprofit Executive*

## ACHI Magazine Award Recipient 2021
*Nonprofit Executive of the Year Award*

*Letitia Council*

Best Selling Author | Speaker

@letitiacouncil    @letitia_council7

## About Me

Letitia Council is an Eastern Shore Native, resides in Portsmouth, Virginia. She has been nominated for Nonprofit Leader with Sister's Leaders Conference, been awarded for Nonprofit Executive Leader 2021 by ACHI Magazine Awards, nominated for Nonprofit Leader, Woman of Influence & Woman on the Rise by ACHI Magazine Awards 2022. She has been featured in Voyage ATL in 2021, featured on the Power Leaders and Grace Show twice, Big Mind Entertainment, seen on Coast Live. Letitia loves to spend time with her loving devoted husband and her amazing children.

Letitia loves to share her story about how Traumatic Brain Injury caused her to lack "Hope" and how TBI and God helped her rise from the ashes of her trauma. Letitia is also the founder of Women on the Move Conference.Uplifting women of many journeys, inspiring them to keep the faith, stay the course and encourage them that Hope isn't lost. Letitia cared for her daughter who sustained a Traumatic Brain Injury in 2019 up until God called her home. Her mission to assist TBI Caregivers is her passion, her purpose and apart of her healing.

## Speaking Topics

▶ *Traumatic Brain Injury*

(TBI) is an "Invisible Disability" Brain injury community that is often underserved and overlooked. To prevent "lack" I speak from a place to increase awareness, education and advocacy.

▶ *Hope in Healing*

Psalm 147:3

He heals the brokenhearted and binds up their wounds.

▶ *Inspiration.*

Letitia loves to share her story and allow God to speak through her as she inspires others that even if their hope is lacking it's not lost. Inspiring others to Rise from the ASHES of Their TRAUMA. Rise up, inspire and GO its not over.

▶ *Grief*

Grief is hard to bear, but it's not the end. Don't let grief consume you to where you are Breathing while Suffocating. You can conquer grief and I am a living witness, yes it still hurts but I can now breathe without Suffocating.

## Featured Speaking Engagements

Power, Leaders & Grace Talk Show / Dawne Horizon Podcast

Community Health & Wellness Fair- / Soul Care Series

Woman Achieving Victory Podcast / Vision Driven 757

Fragrance of Faith Ministry / Sassy Women who Win

## Get In Contact with me Today!

📞 757-541-2329

✉ infotbi2019@gmail.com

🌐 www.letitiacouncil.com

# From Broken Promises to Blessed Purpose

## by Tacole Robinson

I finally said *yes* to God, and was determined to make Him pleased. I made the decision to follow Him and allow Him to transform me for His glory. I stopped partying. I stopped cussing. I stopped having sex. I started fasting and praying. I started studying in seminary. I was all in. Have you ever said *yes* to God? Hopefully, you were not like me. I said *yes* and expected no pain, disappointments, or delays. I concluded that doing things God's way was the best and only way. I had not considered the fact that there might be obstacles and challenges along the way— silly me.

While in seminary, I married my husband. We both were serious about our relationships with God. We were prayerful people, and we trusted God wholeheartedly. That's why after meeting one another one time, we soon married. In less than three months, we exchanged our vows. We had much evidence that God was doing something new and something wonderful for us.

> *Behold, I will do a new thing, now it shall spring forth;*
> *Shall you not know it? I will even make a road in the*
> *wilderness and rivers in the desert.*

— ISAIAH 43:19 KJV

We understood the promise. He was doing something new and doing it now. Did you notice what I did? I missed the part about making a road in the wilderness and the rivers in the desert.

After two years of marriage, we were excited to discover we were expecting a baby. We were so grateful. We wanted children together. When we married, my husband already had two sons. We were looking forward to the blessed opportunity of having children with our shared DNA.

On February 14, 2008, I went to the doctor for my twelve-week visit. The doctor came in so we could listen to the baby's heartbeat. There was no heartbeat. I could not believe it! There was a sac, but it was empty. The doctors did their best to explain to me what was happening with the pregnancy.

I was told that I had a miscarriage and would need to return in a few days to check my HCG level to be sure it was decreasing. At this point in my life, I had great faith! I knew there was nothing impossible with God. I had witnessed God answer many prayers of healing for those whom I'd prayed for. I said *yes* and was serving as needed. Surely, God would turn this situation around for us.

About two weeks after my Valentine's Day news, I found myself in worship. As service began, I was asked to lead the corporate prayer. All of a sudden, I felt a tremendous need to go to the bathroom. As I hurriedly ran to the bathroom and got to the toilet, my precious pregnancy passed into the toilet. I wailed and cried, and wailed and cried. How could this loving God allow this to happen to me? Not to me? I'm the one who said *yes* to the hospital visits, telephone calls, and sending of cards. I'm the one who prayed, fasted, and expected God to work miracles.

Someone overheard my travail and went to get my best friend. She banged on the bathroom door until I let her in. We, somehow, managed to say goodbye to the promise in that small space.

I returned to the sanctuary, just as they called me up to pray. Here I was, again, interceding for others when I desperately needed someone to pray for me.

I had not had the opportunity to share the bathroom experience with my husband. I reminded myself and God that He was a good, good

Father. I chose to focus on a prayer of thanksgiving that morning, even though I felt like my heart was being ripped apart.

The pain of losing that baby was challenging, to say the least. In our excitement, we shared the good news, never thinking we would have to go back and tell everyone about a miscarriage. I wanted to know why, and to find out if any physical hindrances with me would prevent me from conceiving and giving birth.

For some reason or another, I took on the responsibility for this loss. It was my fault in some way or another. The doctors discovered fibroids in my uterus. Some of them were fairly large, and it was suggested that I get surgery to remove them. During this surgery, the doctor discovered an ectopic pregnancy. To remove it, he had to cut one of my tubes, which decreased the possibility of conceiving even more.

Once again, I said *yes* to this process of becoming a mother. I knew in my heart, mind, and spirit that I was created to be a mother. By this time, we had received prophecies related to having children. My husband was told he would have four sons; at that time, he only had two. I was told that I would conceive and that I would have twins. I had the surgery, and we did what married people do. Each month, I was disappointed when my cycle started. I needed a second myomectomy to remove more fibroids that had grown.

I became depressed and angry. To me, it was unfair that I was married and trying to be a "good Christian." Yet, I struggled desperately to get pregnant, let alone stay pregnant. All around me, people were getting pregnant. Women who were not married— pregnant! Women who did not plan to get pregnant— pregnant! Women who did not want to be pregnant— pregnant! In one year, I helped plan four baby showers. I quickly became worn out, especially in the instances of young unmarried women with multiple children. When I received invitations to their baby showers, I did not attend.

It was then that I recalled my desire growing up to be a foster parent. I spent some time in the foster care system and wanted to provide love and safety for a child in need. After convincing my husband that this was a path for me to be a mother, he agreed to learn more about it. God spoke again and reassured us through a dream that this was His will. We endured the process of becoming foster parents and are so glad we did.

We have served many children. Some have stayed for a day, and three are staying forever.

While in a service, I was called out by a prophet of God. He knew my name. He asked for T-a-c-o-l-e Robinson. He told me that God would do for me what I had prayed for others. I would conceive and give birth. This promise brought me much joy and hope. God had not forgotten about me. I was grateful to mother my other children, but there was still a void. I was so sure that I was supposed to have biological children, as well.

I sought the advice of infertility specialists who informed me that I would never conceive on my own. Two opinions advised me to get a hysterectomy and use a gestational carrier. Thank God for Dr. Garcia, who reviewed my case and agreed to try to help me. I will never forget him telling me my case was challenging, but was willing to try. Fibroids were still an issue, along with the cut tube and high ovaries that could not be reached vaginally during IVF. Dr. Garcia had to retrieve my eggs abdominally.

We said *yes* again— this time, to the process of IVF. The first two rounds of IVF were unsuccessful. My body was stressed. My blood pressure was off the charts. I developed shingles. I was sad and depressed. I was ready to throw in the towel.

While attending a women's conference, I heard the Word of the Lord. I heard very clearly, "Try again." My response was, "At your Word, I will try again." God cemented in my heart and mind that "all is well."

We did another round of IVF. I kept confessing, "All is well." From the point of transferring the embryo, I lived my life like I was pregnant. I was very careful of what I did and did not do.

I will never forget Sunday, August 20, 2017. On my husband's birthday, I went to the lab to have my blood drawn for the pregnancy test and then went to church. When church was over, I checked my voicemail messages, where I heard, "Your pregnancy test is positive." I took off running, shouting, and crying. I was so grateful to see my baby's heartbeat on the ultrasound. I kept reminding God of the words of the prophet that I would conceive and give birth. I was hopeful that His promise would come to pass, and that I would not be disappointed again.

I went back to Dr. Garcia for a follow-up. I was probably ten weeks pregnant. He did not see a heartbeat. He immediately sent me for another ultrasound with better machines. Before walking in, I prayed and called my husband and prayer warriors. I recall my husband asking for a Lazarus experience. When the woman turned on the sound, and I heard my baby's heartbeat, I almost broke the table with my reaction. I was so grateful to witness another miracle, but it was for me this time!

This pregnancy was full of scares. I bled almost every day until delivering the baby. I had to comfort myself with the reassuring words of: "All is well." I had to tell myself that all was well, no matter what I saw, heard, or felt.

As we got closer to the end, the doctor ordered more tests to ensure the baby's good health. On one of these visits, when I was thirty-four weeks, they discovered a loss of amniotic fluid. I was admitted to the hospital for observation. By Sunday, I was doing better and was told that I could go home. My doctor wanted me to return the following morning to repeat testing. Something just didn't sit right with me. I was not ready to leave the hospital. I asked the nurse to give me just thirty minutes. She went out to tell the doctor and was back within minutes. She thought the baby may have had decelerations in his heartbeats. Sure enough, she was right. I had an emergency C-section.

When I woke up, the doctor was there in the waiting room. She told us how she had a hard time with the surgery. As soon as she cut into my abdomen, it began to fill with blood. She could not find the baby, and I was losing blood. The doctor said she felt a force take control of her hands, guiding her to the baby. She told us she always wondered if God was real. Now, she knows He is.

Tears streamed down my face, as she shared her experience with us. God had shown up and showed out again. I was so happy to hear that she was acknowledging God. She later told us that she immediately shared the experience with new doctors the following week, when she began teaching them at the hospital. I was also honored to know the details regarding how God had our back. We both could have died during the surgery, but God! He kept His promise. No weapon formed against us shall prosper.

After delivering Malachi, we were grateful. I could not stop thinking about Deja Joy, though. Deja Joy was my baby girl whom I saw in my dreams and visions. A prophetess called me many years ago and told me that God showed her that I would have a baby girl. When we became pregnant with Malachi, I was so sure that this was Deja Joy. Wrong! The baby was a boy, and I could not stop thinking about her.

After healing, we agreed to try IVF again. God did it again, and allowed us to carry another baby. We soon discovered the baby was a girl. This pregnancy was so much different than the previous one. The anxiety was less, and I seemed to be healthier. My blood pressure was well managed.

At thirty-two weeks, I went into the doctor's office for a routine ultrasound. The previous weekend, I had not been feeling well. I felt like I had the flu. I just felt yucky. I did not call the doctor because I had an upcoming appointment. It was not until I was sitting in the waiting area that I began to wonder about the last time I felt Deja Joy move. Soon afterward, they called my name to go back. As she put the probe on my belly, she began to ask how I'd been feeling. As I told her about the weekend, she stopped and said she would be right back. She needed to get the doctor. The doctor came in and confirmed that there was no heartbeat.

I was devastated. I could not believe God would allow this to happen again. We had made it so far. Why would this happen now at thirty-two weeks? The doctor sent me home to wait for him to decide the best course of action regarding the baby's delivery. I had so many questions. I did not know what to expect. Was this really it for Deja Joy, or was God going to do another miracle? We were hopeful for the latter and went into delivery expecting a live baby.

Prior to going into the operating room, I insisted that someone from the NICU be present to care for my miracle baby. I did not want to waste time waiting for them to arrive. To our great disappointment, Deja Joy was dead when she was delivered. This operation was also challenging for the doctors. They had a hard time getting her out of my uterus, and I lost a lot of blood, again.

The pain of losing Deja Joy was inconsolable. I was angry all over again. I did my best to explain to my children where Deja Joy was and why she was not coming home from the hospital with Mommy. I found comfort in the beautiful pictures the nurses took for us. I appreciated the time I was given to hold her, even though I was in the ICU. But that was not enough. I wanted and needed my baby girl to be with me in the flesh. I longed for her. I cried for her.

We had one more frozen embryo left from the cycle with Deja Joy, and there was no way we would ever discard our baby. So, we agreed to try again— one more time. And lo and behold, we were pregnant. We soon found out that we were pregnant with twins! This was the fulfillment of prophecy! We were carrying identical twin boys. We felt like we were living Job's life. God had certainly given us double for our trouble.

At nineteen weeks, I went in for a routine visit. I was quickly sent to the ER when I shared that I had a cough that I could not get rid of. They wanted me to go downstairs and be tested for COVID-19. Before going, I asked the doctor if he could check my babies. He said "No." After getting my results, someone in labor and delivery conducted my checkup. My test was negative, and after five hours, I was finally examined. The doctor left the room to get help. She said she was having difficulty finding both babies, which was not uncommon. They liked to play hide-and-seek. She returned with the midwife, who informed me that there was only one heartbeat.

*God, not again! You have got to be kidding me!* I said *yes*, but it seems like You are the one who is constantly saying *no*!

I was told to go home and wait for the doctor to call me the next morning. I had so many questions. What was I supposed to do? Will I deliver the babies now? Will I miscarry the deceased child only? I left the hospital broken and afraid. I wasn't confident the other child would survive. I was angry and disappointed, again. No one provided support. A social worker was not called. My discharge papers said, "return to routine activities." I was not offered a note for work. I'm sorry, but I just discovered I lost one of my babies. Who in their right mind can go on as if nothing happened? Was I supposed to get up the next morning and teach like my heart was not in shambles?

It was then that I realized there was so much wrong with how grieving parents are cared for. Infertility and fetal losses are often silent hurts. Mothers and fathers are left to grieve on their own. In many instances, others are unaware of their challenges and are often insensitive, though unintentionally. Those who long to hold a child are often questioned about when they will have children or why they haven't started their family. Jobs do not provide bereavement days to heal physically and emotionally. Medical professionals are needed to support and encourage these parents.

My experience with infertility and fetal loss has given me a new passion. What appeared to be broken promises has given me my blessed purpose. I am looking forward to providing a safe place for healing. My pain now has a purpose, and God will get the glory.

# *About the Author*

Elder Tacole Robinson is called to be a mother. There have been many challenges along the way, from infertility to fetal loss. Despite life's circumstances, she has found joy in the presence of a faithful God.

In 2005, she married her husband, Prophet Marlon Robinson. They have five sons and two daughters. As a foster parent, she has learned how to 'love and let go' of medically fragile children who need nurturance, healing, and stability. Together, they have a healing and deliverance ministry through Garden of Glory Ministries.

Elder Robinson desires to study to show herself approved by God; therefore, she is a lifelong learner. She has a Master of Divinity degree from Northern Baptist Theological Seminary and a Master of Education degree from The Ohio State University.

To gain insight into Tacole's journey toward motherhood, grab a copy of her book— *Getting to JOY: A Mother's Journey With Infertility, Miscarriage, and Stillbirth*. She bravely recounts her experiences with infertility, miscarriage, and stillbirth, which unexpectedly led her to find joy. Throughout the pages of this book, her heartfelt intention is to offer support, instill hope, and facilitate healing for individuals who are going through the process of grief.

You can connect with Tacole through her personal ministry, *Tacole Robinson Ministries*, which can be found on all social media platforms and her website: www.tacolerobinson.com.

# I Was On His Mind

## by Taibika Henson-Garnes

*I was on God's mind...*

When I think about some of the challenges I faced in life, I now know that God was with me the whole time. Although some of these challenges result from my choices, God was using it to shape whom I would become. God will use our errors and bad decisions as learning tools, and they will ultimately be used as a testimony for others. There are times when pain is necessary to grow and become whom God has created you to be. Life will take you on many roller coasters, but deciding when to get off is up to you.

I have encountered many challenges throughout life, many caused by the decisions I made without God. I will share a portion of my story and hope that many can benefit and learn from my errors or bad judgment calls.

Being a mother at an early age changed my life in ways I didn't understand, forcing me to grow up quickly. I made mistakes along the way because I wasn't fully finished living my young adult years before I brought another life into the picture. I do not regret having my son because he is a part of me. However, there was a time when my son hated me; he even told me so when he was younger. I didn't understand how he could have hated me because I thought I was a good mother. He eventually told me why, and my heart was broken. He said that I always put other people before him, especially men. I was partying and living my life, not making time for him. During the critical points of his life, I was too busy. There were times when he needed me, and I was preoccupied with other people.

His dad was in his life until he was about ten years old, and then his life ended due to a car accident. My son's life was shattered, but he really didn't show any type of emotion. He cried at the funeral, but he's never really dealt with the loss of his father. At the time of his father's death, I had been married for about two years, and my son was still trying to build a relationship with my husband. It was hard, and my son could not or would not connect with him. It hurt me because I thought that he never would. There were years of confrontation, yelling, and crying. We needed help. I tried finding him a mentoring program for boys, but was told there was a shortage of male mentors.

Our lives changed once we found this Christian summer camp that my son and my niece attended. While attending the camp, God made a divine connection between Apostle Etta Banks and us. She saw something in my son and showed him the love of Christ, even though he was hard to deal with. From that point on, we became members of her church and are now a part of her leadership.

I didn't understand the pain then, but I understand it now. I understand that pain is needed, and we may not like it, but it has a purpose. We don't suffer in vain; God will use your pain for something you could never imagine.

Now that my son is grown and a father, I see major changes in him. He dealt with anger, and I am sure he is still processing it. He's different now, and we get along. We don't argue anymore. Our relationship was not good when he was younger, but everything changed for the better in 2014. I know that God has big plans for him. He has not yet fully given his life over to God, although he is saved. God is still working on his heart, and I have faith that he will be who God has called him to be. I thank God for my husband because through it all, he didn't run. He stayed and took care of his blended family.

He is what I prayed for because his love for me is unconditional. I am his queen, and he is my king; we know how to love and support one another. There has never been any disrespect in our almost fifteen years of marriage. We have had issues, but we allowed God to be at the center of our marriage. So, those issues never consumed our marriage. Even the issues with our son never caused animosity or division between us.

I rejoice at the fact that we decided to become members of New Vision for Life Church, where we have learned so much. God has a plan for everything we go through, and the situations or problems that we encounter. God loves us beyond what we could imagine. Our circumstances are not who God is, and people get mad at God when things don't go their way.

*I was on God's mind...*

I believe that the season that I am in now is God-ordained, and I am embracing what He is doing in my life. We don't always have to know God's plan because this is where we use our faith. The Word says that we walk by faith and not by sight. We won't always see what God is doing, He is God and God alone. He knows what He's doing; we must trust that without seeing it.

When I think about everything I have been through, I know God was with me. I have a greater appreciation and understanding of God's grace. Grace is the free and unmerited favor of God. God extended grace to me that I didn't deserve. He loves me so much that I was on His mind before I was born. There is no love greater than God's love. My heart wants to be right in the eyes of God. I want to make Him happy because He has done great things for me. That unconditional love that He has for me is unexplainable. How could He love me so much? I make mistakes, and don't always do what He says, but He loves me. It's not the same love that people show us. It's a love that I can't explain; I just feel God's love. I see how He walked me through situations that I put myself in. So many bad things could have happened to me, but God saw fit to keep me here on earth. I know God has a plan for me, and I don't have to fear.

When I was younger, God was not on my mind. I wanted to do what I wanted to do. Although God was not on my mind, I was on His.

I wanted to be grown up without my parents telling me what to do. I could not wait until I was an adult. I don't know why. I don't know why we rush to grow up. If we only knew what we know now, we would never rush to grow up.

Thinking about how God changed my life makes me smile. He helped me stay sane in my marriage when my husband's health was not good at the beginning of our marriage. I worked full-time, dealing with our son and his behavior, while managing my husband's care. I took him to the hospital every week, sometimes every other week. It was tremendously overwhelming. God strengthened me and kept me through all of it. There were times when I wanted to run and never look back, but God would not let me. I thanked Him that He would not let me run. I would be missing out on all that God is doing now. I see His hand in my marriage and with our son.

That time of my life felt so lonely. I felt like no one knew what I was going through, not even my family, although they were very supportive. I would ask God, "Why me?" Why did I have to go through this? This was the part that I didn't understand, and I wanted Him to take it away. However, going through all of this made me run into God's arms, and I felt safe there. My relationship grew closer to Him.

I love to write, and I would write in my journals. It gave me peace. God gave me peace during the storm. That's God. He comforts His children. He sees when we cry and when we are going through trials and tribulations, and He will comfort you. He has so much that He wants to show you and share with you, but you must accept it. He will not force you to want Him. That's the choice you must make.

God is not looking for us to be perfect. He wants us to accept His will for our lives. God is not mean; He loves us and wants the best for us. Many times, we have a plan for what we want to do, but if God is not in it, it won't work. We think that we know what is right for us, but we don't. Sometimes, we desire things that aren't good for us, and God knows that. He tries to protect us from things, but some of us push so hard, and our will is all we can hear or see. You may go with what you want and satisfy your flesh, but you are still not satisfied when that moment is over. The Bible should be what we follow because all the answers are there. God knew that we would need to understand how we were created, why we exist, and how to live according to His ways.

Life is only hard if you decide that you want to do things according to your ways. People think that God doesn't care because of everything that happens in the world. The evil of the world is the effect of people choosing not to accept God's will. The thing about it is that the events that happened in the Bible are what we see today. God already knew we would rebel, be disobedient, and choose to do things He told us not to do. Even then, when we are ready to give up the things of the world, God receives us with open arms. He loves us more than we love ourselves and wants to clean us up. I am happy that He wants us back. At some point in our lives, we may realize that we made mistakes, and only He can change our hearts. But we must want the change for ourselves!

We must let Him into our hearts, and allow Him to heal us. People will break our hearts, offend us, betray us, talk about us, cheat, steal, and more. If you don't allow God in, you will become miserable and bitter toward others, even those who didn't do anything to you. God is love, and His love is real. You never have to worry about Him treating you badly. We are a part of Him. He created us in His image and gave us the mind of Christ. We are His children. What good parent doesn't want the best for their kids?"

Satan wants us to go against everything God stands for because he hates Him. The thing about it is that Satan hates us, too, because we are descendants of Christ.

God has a plan for everyone. He has a plan for your pain. Don't always look at pain in a bad way. I am not talking about physical pain. I am talking about the pains of life and the journey that life can take us on. Trust God's plan for your life because you can't go wrong with that. His promises are *yes* and *amen*, and don't return to Him void. He created you with a purpose in mind, and you cannot change God's plan. The best thing to do is accept it and know that suffering is a part of life, but it's easier with God. With God, you are never alone. His Word says that He will never leave you nor forsake you. I know, at times, you may feel that God is distant, but He's not distant. It feels that way because you changed position. The things you are facing and your disobedience caused you to walk away from God. You can ask God for forgiveness, repent, and turn to Him for direction and guidance for your life.

Submitting to God is the best option for your life because He knows exactly what you need. Allowing Him into your heart and accepting Him as your Lord and Savior will help you in your walk with Christ. Understanding that His ways are different from ours and His thoughts are different from ours, will stop you from trying to figure God out. He will do things we simply won't understand, but know there is a reason for them. Know that He has your best interest in mind. He created you, and He knows everything about you. He knows what you are thinking and what you will say before you say it.

He is not a dictator, and He gives you a choice. However, know that there are consequences for your actions. He will forgive you for your sin, actions, thoughts, and words, but you must repent and turn away from those things. We all have a story to share, and when people share, take heed to it. It's up to you to receive what they share, and if you are struggling with similar problems, please never think it cannot happen to you. God will show you how to love others as He loves you.

Remember that nothing you do can make God stop loving you. His love is constant, and it never changes. No matter how many mistakes and times you fall, He still loves you.

> *"Behold, I have engraved you on the palms of my hands. Your walls are continually before me."*
>
> — ISAIAH 49:16 ESV

That means He cannot forget you because you are in His hands!

## *About the Author*

Taibika Henson-Garnes was born and raised in Baltimore, MD. She is a mother, wife, published author, leader, certified pharmacy technician, and armor bearer to her pastor, Apostle Etta Banks. In 2014, she published her first book, *Released from My Past and Birthed Into My Destiny*. This book is a testimony of her past and how God delivered and set her free. In 2020, she was a co-author of a book called *Woman of Virtue: Walking in Excellence, Volume 2*. Her vision is to see people being healed and delivered from their past. Everyone has a story, and it's time we share it to help others in their healing process.

# Sticks and Stones

## by Linda Harvey

E tymology is the origin of a word, and the historical development of its meaning. Proper word use is essential in creating a safe foundation for thoughts, concepts, and ideas. For a developing child, words that nurture and are pleasing to the ear become tools in how that child sees himself or herself, the people who shape their lives, and the world around them.

In the book of Proverbs, I found several scriptures that support my thoughts for this chapter:

Kind words are like honey— *sweet to the soul* and *healthy* for the body.
— Proverbs 16:24 NLT, emphasis mine

Wise words satisfy like a *good meal*; the right words bring *satisfaction*.
— Proverbs 18:20 NLT, emphasis mine

Like *golden apples set in silver* is a word spoken at the right time.
— Proverbs 25:11 ISV, emphasis mine

## SMOOTH STONES

The words of my father gave me confidence, causing me to take joyful strides prompting an "I can do it" mindset. The sky was the limit! His words validated and affirmed me, boosting my personal growth and self-confidence. His words had value and were like gems nestled in a golden crown. They became the smooth stones I used to create the many paths in life.

The words of my mother gave me the ability to see the girl in the mirror. I enjoyed the days when she'd plait my hair and tie the strings of my romper gently upon my shoulders. A mother's words, like smooth stones, help build self-worth. Her words were likened to pearls beautifully strung that adorned my life with grace.

The smooth stones, words of wisdom and encouragement, even as a young child, enabled me to see and grasp the world around me. Without hesitation, I'd lift my face toward the sun to feel its warmth while squinting my eyes – enjoying a world without a gate.

## OIL FOR LANTERNS

A good word spoken from a caring heart is like a brick that helps build a good foundation. A word that inspires the soul is embraced like the warmth of a spring breeze. A grandmother's words are likened to the golden apple set in silver— a good word released at the right time.

My grandmothers' words of wisdom also perfumed the chapters of my life. I was often comforted by their love and support. I rejoice, thinking of the time spent with my grandmothers, especially after I inherited my mother's old blue Maverick.

My grandfathers' words made me curious because they spoke from rich and sometimes adventurous experiences. I would sit and listen because the golden nuggets of wisdom, sometimes fueled by laughter, were still an intricate part of my life.

The spoken words of my ancestors are like a beautifully woven quilt. Each patch of fabric— a memory, imagery, laughter, chat, and whispers from times past— is a window I look through often. Their words painted the canvas of my life— the shadows of souls resting and the voices of those present were the stones and oil for my lantern.

I felt confident that life would never throw a curveball. Once upon a time, in my utopian view, I could never imagine my world changing, but it did. The whimsical dance was ending—an ode to childhood. The warmth of the sun changed, and there was a need for a gate— something to protect my heart.

*Words change* as seasons in life change.
*Words change* as you navigate through the bumpy ride of puberty.
*Words change* as people in your life enter and exit.
*Words change* as your personal experiences become tabletop chats.
*Words change* as friendships dissolve without resolution.
*Words change* when those you love endure hardships, grief, and loss.
*Words change* as loved ones transition into death.
*Words change* as friends embrace other interests and relationships.
*Words change* when you realize you made poor life choices.
*Words change* when love fades, and the dance on the gilded floor ends.

Words change... *I know.*

The misuse of words can be quite devastating and life-altering. Words rendered with impure intentions pierce the heart, confuse the mind, bruise the spirit, and deeply wound the soul.

A quote by Herbert Spencer says, "How often misused words can generate misleading thoughts." Another quote rings true by Margaret Heffernan: "Words are how people think. When you misuse words, you diminish your ability to think clearly and truthfully."

## WORDS BECAME WEAPONS

Harsh words are like an old 45 record that can't move forward because the needle is unable to glide past the scratch in the vinyl. In its desperate attempt to play the song, the record sticks, and the same lyrics play over and over, like the harsh words that met me years ago. Those harsh words became an imprint on my mind. Just one word— a statement—

changed the trajectory of how I felt about myself. Words seemed to bully me; they were relentless. I became the old 45 record, unable to move past the scratch on my heart.

Proverbs, 12:18a (NCV) states, "Careless words *stab like a sword*" (emphasis mine), and Proverbs 15:4b (NLV) says, "A deceitful tongue *crushes the spirit*" (emphasis mine).

I was spiritually and emotionally disabled. Instead of pushing the words away, I embraced them. They became fused to my soul, taking root, only to feed on the other words that caused me to weep. My mind was cluttered and unable to extract the stinging language. I was always in pain.

The ability of speech is a gift from God. In the book of Genesis, we see God as the Creator. Through His spoken words, He created galaxies, celestials, vegetation, cattle, humanity, and much more. And God said, "Let there be..." (Genesis1:1-31 NIV). Whatever God called forth was well thought out, fully created, and firmly established.

Let's think about this: What words have we spoken that were carefully thought out? How were those words, phrases, and statements delivered? Were they helpful? What did they create? You see, over time, I understood the value of words. They can inspire, isolate, cause victories, or kill like venom. The stinging language of words spoken would either validate or victimize me.

"Sticks and stones may break my bones, but words will never hurt me."

*That was a lie.*

## STICKS

Words expressed caused me to feel loved, valued, and safe. My journey was influenced by the individuals who were part of my journey. Their words strummed the cords of my self-belief, self-worth, and overall trust.

Over time, words that made me feel good somehow became sinister and dark. The melody of words expressed changed like a boomerang; words would leave but never return in the same manner. Life changes, people change, and ideas change. It's exceptionally harder when those you love and trust change, and their words become suspect. Why did you say that to me? What does that mean? Now, how should I feel?

*Words that Crush*

I remember playing hopscotch with one of my childhood friends, one of our favorite outdoor games. While playing, she whispered to another friend that I was ugly. It was the first time anyone described me that way. I was puzzled, especially since I was going through the "ugly duckling" stage that already had me on edge. That type of experience continued through Middle and High school; it was hurtful, and I tried my best to push it away. All sorts of words followed my life; some buzzed in my ears, others hitched a ride on my back, and a few took on some form of life.

Something strange happens when words become weapons – you start fighting back! *An eye for an eye...a tooth for a tooth...a word for a word*! This was just like the sticks from my grandmother's shrub that we peeled to hit each other while playing. Afterwhile, the hit and the evidence of a whelp were no longer fun. Words that become the stinging language many of us have experienced and have not dealt with will leave whelps on your heart and soul.

A quote by Ranal Currie says, "If you are using words to hurt others, you are misusing them."

"Words have power."
— *Forbes*

"Words are free; how you use them may cost you."
— *Quotesgram*

I was pregnant with words authored by others, coupled with my own thoughts. The stinging language with its taunting lyrics became part of what I believed and wore like an oversized winter coat. Perhaps I thought, I am what the chatter suggests— ugly, dumb, and worthless.

Just like that old 45 record, I could not move past the scratch on my heart. Mirror, mirror, on the wall, how many times must I stall?

## STONES

As a young woman, words from my past fit around me like a child's glove— restricting. They wrapped around my thoughts, ideas, and plans like the web of a spider. I realized some choices made in life were the result of what I heard, and ultimately believed.

**words** that screamed obscenities
**words** that cursed and shamed
**words** that were violent and fear-provoking
**words** that made me shudder and shrink
**words** spewed like spikes by the one who sang the sacred hymns!
**words** from twisted lips claiming, "I will protect you!"
**words** spoken by dancing eyes professing, "I will always love you!"
**words** that painted the contour of my cheeks with untimely tears

Their words did not measure up!

The stones, no longer smooth, were jagged and rough. Words that soothed and comforted, now intentionally crude and cold. So, I used their jagged words against them and built a fortress around my heart! Why me? How did I manage to get through the darkest times in my life? Sexual abuse? Poor self-esteem! Domestic trauma? Suicide? Poor self-worth!

So, in my defense— and yes, defiance— I struck back using the very words that haunted me. Their lyrics came from the stinging language; their words were used as a weapon. Rising like a wounded Phoenix from the pit of trauma, I found *a* voice. My *words* became sticks and stones.

For a time, my stony expressions felt like a shield. I deliberately executed words that caused tears and kept people at a distance. But my life was evolving, and it became difficult to wear the weighted armor. In the midst of my misery, God heard my cry and responded. He began to send people who were unbothered by my crude tactics. You see, they truly understood my story, for they, too, knew the lyrics of the stinging language. Those were the same words that ushered them into downward spirals of emotional anguish and loneliness. In their kind efforts, I found a way to navigate from the pain of my past to a more purposeful and promising future. This time, I would not allow the lyrics, vamps, and words of my past to dictate my next steps. Guided by God and my regained strength, I would focus on a new day— a future I would create.

In a conversation with my grandmother one day, just out of the blue, I asked her how she handled life issues— you know— the storms in life. How did she handle unpleasant relationships? What did she learn? How did she handle mistakes? How do you acknowledge your own faults and forgive those who hurt you? In her response, she was honest. Her words of wisdom were pretty practical, yet encouraging:

- Put a face on the pain.
- Challenge yourself to face it.
- Talk it out, and do not be afraid to cry.
- Turn the words that hurt into words that help.
- You can always fix mistakes.
- Forgiving people is not as hard as you think it is.
- Fill your heart and mind with good words.
- Be at peace with your personal decisions.
- Not everyone will agree with you.
- Limit anything that causes stress in your life.
- Pray and talk to God about it.

Like the golden apples set in silver, my grandmother's wisdom came at the right time.

Traumatic experiences that are active in the lives of others can influence and impact how we feel about ourselves and the world around us. I realized that some levels of vicarious or secondary trauma, and even the personal trauma I suffered, blurred my perception of life. Even though there were wonderful smooth stones and oil for my lantern (wisdom and affirmations) in the early years from my family, what I suffered and believed about myself also shaped my life. So, I decided to take my pain and the shame of my past and turn it into purpose, with God's help.

## BAND-AID PEOPLE

It's true, and most of the time, it's not intentional. When we allow the trauma of our past to take siege and hold us captive, it's difficult to have any type of healthy relationship. Relationships with family, friends, and even God are placed on hold. Those horrid words that took root and flourished over time can be dealt with. I also recognized a conscious and unconscious cultivating of my own words— seed words of mistrust, disappointment, anger, discord, and even unforgiveness. Hurt people hurt people, and embracing the truth is essential for healing.

> *"Be mindful when it comes to your words. A string of some that don't mean much to you, may stick with someone else for a lifetime."*
>
> — RACHEL WOLCHIN

> *"Handle them carefully, for words have more power than atom bombs."*
>
> — PEARL STRACHAN HURD

> *"Words have energy and power with the ability to help, to heal, to hinder, to hurt, to harm, to humiliate, and to humble."*
>
> — YEHUDA BERG

> *"The tongue has no bones, but is strong enough to break a heart. So be careful with your words."*
>
> — UNKNOWN

*"Don't mix bad words with your bad mood. You'll have*
*many opportunities to change a mood, but you'll never*
*get the opportunity to replace the words you spoke."*

— UNKNOWN

A quote by Joel Osteen said it best: "Be careful what you say. You can say something hurtful in ten seconds, but then years later, the wounds are still there."

During my healing, I discovered my own strength and resilience! My father's words remain, and those of my mother still perfume my life. My grandfathers' humor and my grandmothers' wisdom sweetly adorn my soul. The unfortunate circumstances others suffered were not my story, but they impacted my life. Thousands of children are born daily into situations they are too young to understand. What their eyes capture becomes pictorial, and what their ears embrace becomes melodic. We absorb the environment around us that sometimes dictates, without permission, what we become. But we can change the narrative!

You can rise from the ashes of trauma and change the tear-soaked pages of your story to testimonies of triumph. Prayer and walking by faith in God are the keys to freedom! "So, if the son sets you free, you are free indeed" (John 8:36 NIV).

Dear reader, today, you can begin to heal. No matter what has transpired in your life that has caused you to see through a lens of pain, this can change today. How? Face the hurt and silence the stinging language. You will never know how strong you are until you take courage and healing by the hand. It's time to enjoy the life God intended.

Sticks and stones may break my bones, but words ***cannot***...

# About the Author

*Her Grace, Apostle Dr. Linda M. Johnson-Harvey*
*"Serving the Community with the Love of Christ"*

Apostle Dr. Linda M. Johnson-Harvey is the Visionary, Founder, and Overseer for Fragrance of Faith Ministry, Incorporated, a 501(c)3 spirit-led organization that has received numerous citations and awards for leadership and the support of marginalized communities. She serves as the Apostolic Covering for several ministries, programs, and businesses in Maryland, North Carolina, New Jersey, and Virginia.

She celebrates 33 years in ministry, and is a published book author, psalmist, and mentor. She also serves as a Trauma Facilitator and Coach (Trauma Healing Institute) and is a graduate of the very first Storyteller Group for House of Ruth Maryland. In addition, she is a facilitator/mentor for the Maryland Business Roundtable for Education (MBRE) and a member of the Baltimore City Public School Advisory Board. Committed to assisting Chesapeake Bible College and Seminary, she serves as an instructor at the Freedom Temple AME Zion Church satellite center.

Apostle Dr. Harvey continued her educational pursuit and enrichment at Chesapeake Bible College & Seminary and St. Mary's Ecumenical Institute. Furthermore, she is employed at The Johns Hopkins Hospital in Baltimore and celebrates ten years of professional service.

She has spearheaded impactful projects and programs, including:

- Voice of the Village Adopt-a-Family Project
- Baby & Bottles Program
- Heart Talk-Real Talk Program for Women of Faith, Business and Community
- Help Us – Help Them Adopt-a-Family for Thanksgiving (COVID Relief Initiative)
- Help Us – Help Them Adopt-a-Family for Christmas (COVID Relief Initiative)
- The Linda Harvey Ministries, LLC

Apostle Dr. Harvey is excited to officially announce her new 501(c)3 organization— *HOPE Community Service, Inc.* This organization was created to provide deeper service and more tangible resources for disenfranchised communities.

She has received various awards for leadership, including:

- Baltimore City Mayoral Citations for Leadership
- Baltimore City Council Board Leadership Citations
- The Baltimore City Sheriff's Office for Community Engagement
- The East Baltimore Transformation Team for Community Leadership
- The prestigious Dr. Martin Luther King, Jr. Community Service Award
- Citations from the Office of the States Attorney – Marilyn Mosby, Esquire
- The Johns Hopkins Hospital "Pastor Sandy Johnson Community of Care Award"
- Baltimore Mentors Appreciation Award (special luncheon for all Baltimore Mentors)

Apostle Dr. Linda Harvey is the recent recipient of an Honorary Doctorate from the School of the Great Commission

(Eastern Shore Satellite Campus) a fully accredited, international organization. She was dubbed a "trailblazer" in the community and Christian Education.

Apostle Dr. Linda Harvey is grateful and humbled by the recognized work celebrated over the years. She is steadfast in expressing, "*I can't do what I do without my leaders, members, and volunteers.*" She also serves as a spiritual mother and advisor for her spiritual sons and daughters in various states. She remains humbled by the many years of serving the Body of Christ and remains consistent in her quest to build the Kingdom of God and reach all with the Gospel of Christ.

Apostle Dr. Harvey is often celebrated for her infectious personality, style, and dedicated years of serving communities facing the greatest challenges. She has witnessed the miracles of God working in the mission fields which has gladdened her heart.

In the '80s, Apostle Dr. Harvey was deeply involved with demonstrations against gun violence and childhood hunger. She joined hundreds in forging a synergy and walks in Washington, DC to ensure the group's voices were heard against escalating societal issues. Some policies to assist families are in place today because she joined movements for change and other voices that cried aloud campaigning for change.

Apostle Dr. Harvey's life has been one of service. She is truly at her best serving those who cannot return the favor. She's occasionally heard giving praise to members of her family, especially her grandmothers (both licensed missionaries). At age seven, Apostle Dr. Harvey traveled with them to serve the elderly in Maryland and Pennsylvania. Those years of travel and working at her home church (Mt. Olive Baptist) perfumed her steps and formulated a rich and clear understanding of the God-purpose and the calling upon her life.

Apostle Dr. Harvey is the mother of a beautiful and gifted daughter, Tiara who is currently preparing to graduate from Coppin State University – an honor leader and summa cum laude honor student.

She firmly believes that "*everyone has the ability to change community.*"

She echoes a familiar expression from one of her chosen historical mentors, the late Mary Church Terrell, who was the first African Amer-ican woman to earn a degree and national activist for civil rights and women's suffrage: "*Keep everlastingly at it.*"

*"No longer bound on the shores of shame and sorrow*
*I rise as a mighty Phoenix strengthened by the Love of God*
*Beautifully adorned in confidence — fastened by resilience.*
*My life is perfumed by the hope of a new day — the day I created."*

*Strong women wear their pain like stilettos.*
*No matter how much it hurts, all you see is the beauty of it.*

—Harriet Morgan

Made in the USA
Middletown, DE
28 October 2023

41389154R10046